D1389337

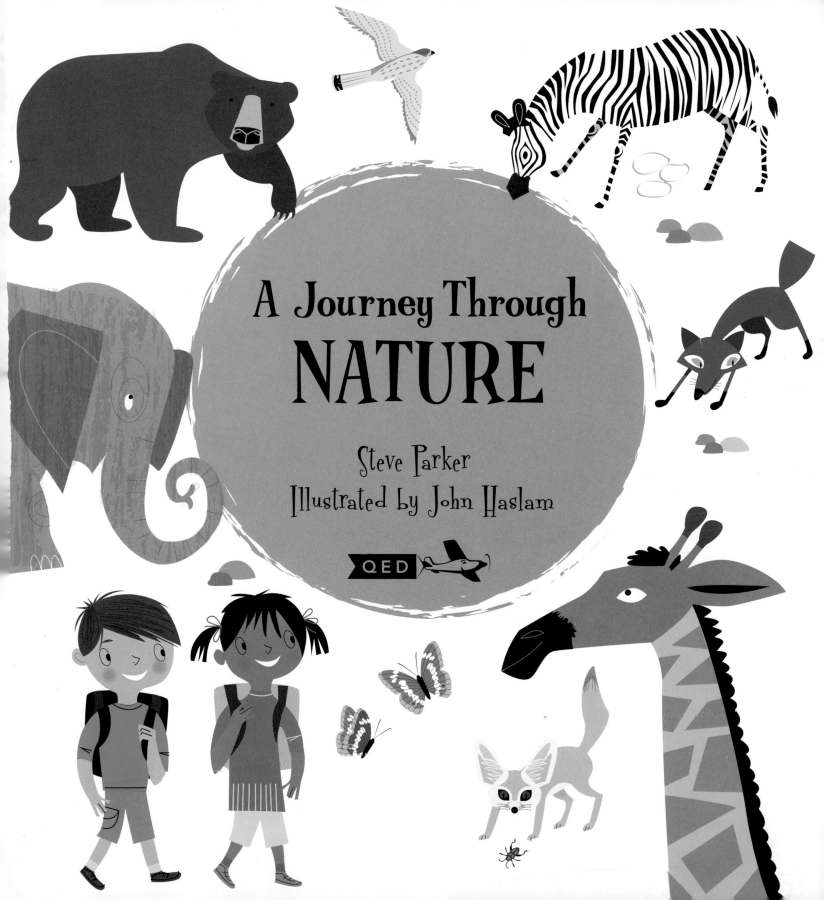

A Journey Through
NATURE

Steve Parker

Illustrated by John Haslam

QED

Copyright © Marshall Editions 2016
Part of The Quarto Group
The Old Brewery, 6 Blundell Street,
London, N7 9BH

First published in the UK in 2016 by QED Publishing

A catalogue record for this book is available from the British Library.

ISBN 978 1 78493 449 1 (hardback edition)

Publisher: Zeta Jones
Associate Publisher: Maxime Boucknooghe
Art Director: Susi Martin
Editorial Director: Laura Knowles
Production: Nikki Ingram
Consultant: Michael Bright

Originated in Hong Kong by
Cypress Colours (HK) Ltd
Printed and bound in China by Toppan Leefung Printing Ltd.
10 9 8 7 6 5 4 3 2 1   16 17 18 19 20

Contents

Let's go outside!

What a lovely day! The sun is shining, the flowers are blooming, the birds are singing and the bees are buzzing. Let's go outside and see what we can find!

The world is full of so many incredible animals and plants. Join us on a fabulous journey to discover the different places where they live.

In the city

Even in towns and cities, nature is never far away. In most countries, pigeons strut around the streets and parks, pecking at crumbs. They nest on the roofs and ledges of buildings.

In North American towns, the raccoon scampers up trees, over fences and across roofs. Its den may be in a tree, under a shed or even in the roof of a house. Its babies are called kits.

In Australia, the possum is well known for stealing garden fruits and vegetables. The baby possum lives in its mother's pouch for five months.

In South America, small monkeys called marmosets climb among city trees and buildings. They feed on all kinds of plant foods. The mother marmoset usually has twin babies.

Along the river

The river is full of life. The big, strong pike hides in waterweeds. When a small fish or frog goes past, the pike races to grab it in its huge mouth.

Swans nest on a quiet part of the river. The mother gives her chicks a ride. The father gives a fierce peck if any animals come near.

The otter family live in a riverside burrow. They swim, twisting and turning, to catch a fish in the water, then bring it out on the bank to eat.

The kingfisher sits on a branch over the water, watching for fish. It dives in like an arrow to seize the fish in its sharp beak.

The catfish has long feelers on its chin. Swimming along the bottom, it stirs up the mud to find food such as worms and water bugs.

At the seashore

Along the coast, gulls circle overhead, searching for food. *Scree! Scraw!* They call noisily to each other as they soar in the wind.

The gulls have webbed feet to help them paddle in the sea and walk across the soft sand.

The crab has strong, sharp claws and a hard shell to protect its insides. It scuttles sideways between the rocks.

A group of seals rest on the sand. They have a thick layer of fat under their skin. This keeps them warm when they swim in the cold sea, looking for fish.

In the rock pool, clusters of mussels cling to the rocks. A beautiful anemone gently waves its tentacles in the warm salt water.

On the cliffs

Look up at the cliffs – animals make their homes here too!

Puffins nest in burrows along the grassy cliff top. They bring back small fish for their chicks, carrying 10 or more at a time.

Gannets nest on the cliff slope in huge groups called colonies. There could be more than 50,000 of them, flapping and squawking.

The stoat is a clever climber. It scrambles up or down the rocks to steal a bird egg, which makes a big feast for its family.

The guillemot lays its egg on the bare rock of a narrow cliff ledge. The egg's pointed shape stops it rolling off.

Huge waves crash into the base of the cliff. Only very tough animals can survive here, such as limpets clinging to the rocks.

Across the desert

Life is hard in the desert. It is hot in the day, cold at night, and very dry. But even here, creatures are able to make it their home.

The biggest desert animals are camels. They only need a drink every week or so – but then they gulp down almost a bathful!

14

Camels have a hump that contains squishy fat. They can use up this store of fat when they can't find food, or use it to make water inside their bodies.

The fennec fox's huge ears pick up the tiny sounds of its food, such as mice, small lizards and even beetles and ants.

Beware of any snake! The horned viper has a bite that is deadly to mice, rats and birds – and perhaps to people as well.

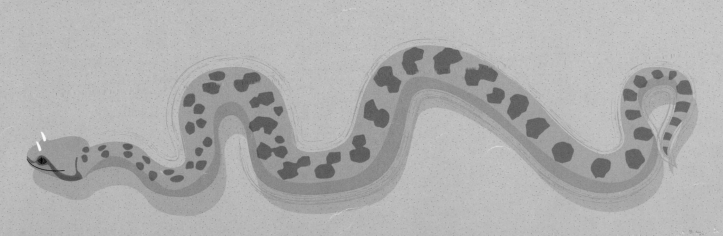

On the grasslands

Time to go on safari — how many animals can you spot? The zebra herd has spent hours eating grass. They watch, listen and sniff the air. At any sign of danger, they will gallop away.

Elephants are the world's biggest land animals. They chew grass and leaves on the African grasslands. The oldest female is the leader of the family.

The lion family is called a pride. The male has a mane of hair around his head.

The female lions feed their cubs on milk. Soon the cubs will be ready to hunt.

The ostrich has small wings and it cannot fly, but it has long legs and runs as fast as a racehorse.

It is the father, not the mother, that guards the baby chicks in their nest.

Into the rainforest

The warm, damp tropical rainforest is packed with many different animals.

The higher branches, twigs, leaves and flowers are called the canopy. Most creatures live here, such as bugs, frogs, lizards, monkeys, sloths, parrots and toucans.

The spider monkey can hang by its tail and travel easily from tree to tree. It screeches and barks to make itself heard.

Among the lower branches and creepers are all kinds of creatures, from beautiful butterflies to fearsome big cats. The jaguar sneaks along a branch.

At ground level, the rainforest has many lakes, rivers and pools. Here lurk big animals such as caimans, big snakes, capybaras and giant fish.

The caiman looks like a crocodile and has an enormous bite. The capybara is a cousin of a pet guinea pig, but is about the size of a family dog.

Up the mountain

Trees grow on the mountain's lower slopes. Above are grassy meadows, then loose rocks, with snow and ice at the top. High up, a mountain becomes colder and windier. Animals have to be tough to live here.

Large deer go up to grassy meadows to feed by day, then come back to the shelter of the trees.

Grey wolves roam all over the mountain. They look for any kinds of food, from rats and rabbits to big deer, which they attack as a pack.

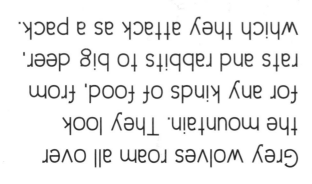

Ptarmigan have patchy brown feathers in the summer. When winter arrives, they grow white feathers to match the colour of the snow.

Bighorn sheep really do have huge horns! The males are called rams. They bash heads with loud bangs. They are trying to show who is the strongest among them.

Among the treetops

Just as many creatures live in the trees as on the ground. The green woodpecker feeds on ants. It uses its strong beak to peck out holes in trees where it builds its nest.

Purple emperor butterflies flit among the treetop branches. They find a sunny patch to show off their shiny colours and attract a mate.

The treecreeper bird walks up tree trunks and along branches. It pecks into the bark for grubs, caterpillars, beetles, flies and spiders.

Tree bumblebees make their nest in a tree-trunk hole. More than 300 of them live inside. They collect nectar and pollen from flowers nearby.

Through the woods

In springtime, the brown bear wakes up from its winter sleep. It comes out of its den to look for food.

The hungry bear likes to eat nuts and berries, and sometimes fish.

High up in a hollow tree, the owl sleeps. When night time comes, it will fly away to hunt for its dinner.

Squirrels run up and down the branches, collecting nuts. They bury some nuts in the ground to keep them safe for winter.

A family of deer nibbles on grass and young leaves. The colour of their fur helps them to stay hidden from danger. The trees give them shelter from the rain.

25

Into the lake

The freshwater turtle has no teeth. It uses its sharp-edged mouth to chop up food.

Its strong shell protects its body, and tough skin with hard scales protects its head and legs.

The young dragonfly, called a nymph, is a fierce hunter of baby fish, tadpoles and water bugs.

Soon it will crawl up a plant stem into the air, wriggle out of its old skin and unfold the wings beneath.

Frogs leap and swim by kicking with their long back legs.

Their big eyes watch for flies buzzing past. The frog flicks out its long tongue to grab the fly and swallows it in one gulp.

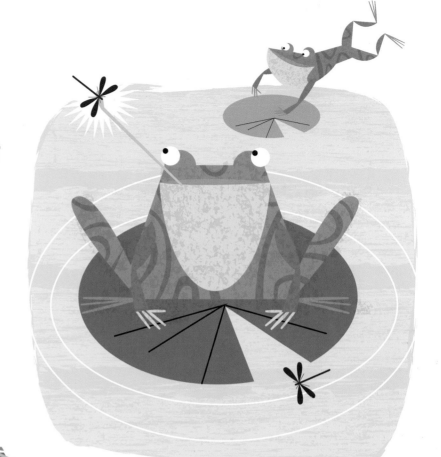

In the middle of the lake, beavers pile up branches and mud to build a house called a lodge.

The lodge keeps them safe and warm. The entrance hole is hidden under the water.

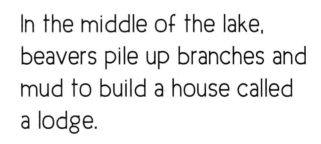

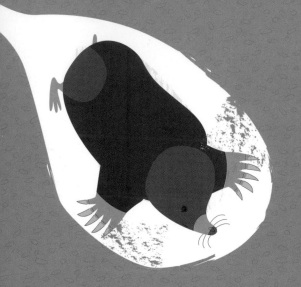

Under the ground

Even underground, nature is keeping busy!

In Europe, the mole digs tunnels with its wide front feet. It pushes up earth and makes molehills, then eats any small creatures it finds.

In Africa, naked mole-rats live in a maze of tunnels. They dig using their large front teeth and feed on underground plant parts like roots and bulbs.

In North America, the sand skink wriggles through sand and loose soil.

In Australia, the platypus digs a burrow into the riverbank. It makes a nest of grass and moss at the end.

All around the world, earthworms tunnel through soil. They let in light, water and nutrients, which help plants to grow. They are called 'nature's gardeners'.

Through fields and hedges

The land where people farm food
is also a home to wildlife.

The kestrel swoops across the meadow
in search of mice and voles.

Hares dash across the fields. They are
such fast runners that few predators
can catch them.

Voles are similar to mice but with short tails.
They scurry along the ground, looking for
grass stems, leaves and seeds to nibble.

The skylark flies from field to field, and lands to peck on seeds and other plant food.

The weasel is a fast and fierce hunter. It chases after rabbits and other small animals.

The dormouse sleeps all winter in a cosy nest among roots. In spring it is very hungry and eats buds, young leaves and bugs.

Across the tundra

As we journey north, we reach the freezing tundra. The land becomes cold and icy.

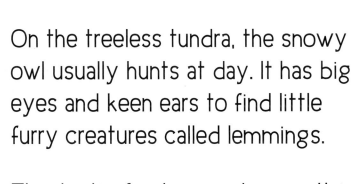

On the treeless tundra, the snowy owl usually hunts at day. It has big eyes and keen ears to find little furry creatures called lemmings.

The Arctic fox has no den or other home. It stays out in the open all winter, which is colder than a home freezer. The fox's extra-thick fur keeps it warm and cosy.

Lemmings shelter in their burrows but come out to eat plants. They have lots of babies – up to ten new babies every month!

Musk oxen scrape away snow with their hooves to nibble the low tundra plants.

Over the ice

In the far north of the world is the Arctic – an ocean covered with floating sheets of ice.

The polar bear has thick fur and huge, hairy paws. It swims and walks many miles to find a seal for a meal.

The male narwhal has one long tooth that sticks out as a tusk. The narwhal uses it to detect what is in the water and look for food.

In the far south of the world is a frozen land surrounded by an icy ocean – the Antarctic.

Killer whales and leopard seals swim among the icebergs, looking for food. The leopard seals hunt for penguins, fish and smaller seals.

On land, emperor penguins walk many miles to their breeding places, where the male looks after the egg until it hatches.

Down into the sea

If you could journey deep
down into the oceans,
you would see some
amazing creatures.

The sperm whale
is the world's
biggest hunter.
It holds its breath
and dives into
the deep ocean for
more than one hour to
catch squid and fish.

The giant squid has a body as big
as a car. Its long tentacles have
strong suckers to grab fish and
other prey.

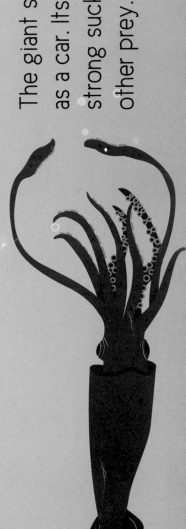

The basking shark swims slowly with its mouth open, taking in all kinds of small shrimps, fish and other small creatures.

The giant spider crab has a body bigger than a dinner plate, and pincers longer than a person's arms.

The gulper eel is almost all mouth! When it opens its mouth wide, it can swallow a creature bigger than itself.

Among the coral reefs

Tropical coral reefs grow in warm, sunny, shallow seas. They are built by creatures called coral polyps. Each one is smaller than a fingertip and makes a hard, shell-like cup around itself.

Coral polyps and anemones open their stinging tentacles to catch tiny creatures, but the clownfish lives safely among the anemones. Its thick, slimy covering prevents it being stung.

The blacktip reef shark swims over the reef. It chases after any fish that leave the safety of the rocks.

The moray eel hides in a cave or crack. It has sharp teeth and a very fast bite.

39

Through the mangroves

In warm places, mangrove trees line the seashore and grow their roots into the mud.

The tiger likes to cool off in the shallow water.

Proboscis monkeys live in the branches. They eat so many leaves that half of their weight can be their full stomach!

Lemon sharks come from the open sea to the mangroves to have their babies. The young sharks stay here for a few years, feeding on small fish.

At low tide, mudskippers use their front fins to hop and jump between the pools.

41

Into the night

As the sun sets, the daytime animals hide away and go to sleep. Now it's the night-time animals' turn to come out.

Bats catch flying insects like moths and gnats. They listen to their own squeaks bouncing back to find their way, even on the darkest night.

In Madagascar, the aye-aye clambers through the trees looking for supper. It uses its good hearing and long, spindly fingers to find tasty grubs underneath the bark.

On African grasslands, the hyaena sniffs and listens as it hunts hares, antelopes and gazelles. The porcupine munches plant food slowly. Its long, sharp quills mean few creatures dare attack it.

In many towns and cities, the red fox sneaks out at night to gobble up leftover food from rubbish bins. Foxes raise their cubs in special holes called dens.

In the countryside or the city, on the land or in the sea, in the bright day or darkest night, nature is all around us.

Can you spot these animals?

Can you work out what they are?

Quiz time!

Can you answer these questions about nature? Here's a hint – you can find all the answers in this book.

1. What do otters eat?

2. What is inside a camel's hump?

3. Where do clownfish live?

4. How does an Arctic fox keep warm?

5. What is the highest part of a rainforest called?

6. What kind of shark swims with its mouth wide open?

7. Which funny-looking creature digs using its big front teeth?

8. Which animal builds a house called a lodge?